Brooklyn
MOM & POP

Written by
Karen McBurnie & Jon Hammer

CONTENTS   ① ② ③ ④ ⑤ ⑥   Neighbourhoods

A neighbourly note
Some readers will have noticed that we use neighbor, the American spelling, on the cover; to do otherwise felt inappropriate. Within the text we use the English spelling of neighbour — and everything else.

NORTH
BROOKLYN

Circo's Pastry

This handsome Sicilian bakery has served Bushwick since 1945. Biscotti and cannoli are terrific, as is the homemade gelati. Wedding cakes and other special occasion desserts are their strong suit. Owner Nino Pierdipino started baking at Circo's in 1966 and his sons have now joined him. The bad old days of the 1970s wiped out much of the best of Bushwick, so it is heartening to see this survivor thriving. The gorgeous neon signage alone is worth the trip.

→ **312 KNICKERBOCKER AVENUE**
☎ **TEL:** *718 381 2292*

▯ **MON:** *9am-4pm*
  TUE-SAT: *8am-7pm*
  SUN: *8am-6pm*

Introduction

"Mom & Pop" as we use the term here, is an affectionate umbrella covering much more than genealogical family; these are small businesses that have thrived over time by working hard for the pride of a job well done, and with the love and patronage of neighbours, friends, and family.

These are not museum pieces, and renovations are not always a matter of choice. Sure, we'd like everyplace to look as it did in the year of its birth, but sometimes practicality wins out over physical attributes; what's important is the continuity of the business and its continuing value in the community.

These are all beloved spots that have helped to define the borough, the Mom & Pop shops folks grew up with, and the places they return to year after year, even if they have moved out of the neighbourhood. There are no substitutes, you won't find an outpost at the mall.

It's not like the old days, and yet it is.

Advisory note: Please note that a good number of establishments listed here are cash businesses and do not accept plastic, Apple Pay, Bitcoin or beads.

Green Farms Supermarket

As Greenpoint slowly but inevitably follows Williamsburg into a characterless monoculture, the Polish shops and restaurants begin to disappear. One stalwart is Green Farms, on the main stretch of Manhattan Avenue, which since 1977 has provided local and imported items at winning prices. In this small supermarket you'll find Polish flours for your baking, a variety of canned and jarred fish, juices, big tubs of fresh pickles and sauerkraut, locally made pierogi, and Eastern European beer. Up front near the register is a meat counter abounding with kielbasi, other sausages and hams, and fresh breads.

-> **918 MANHATTAN AVENUE**

☎ **TEL:** *718 389 4114*

☐ **MON SAT.** *7am-8pm*
   SUN: *9am-3pm*
   CASH ONLY

Irene's / Capri Social Club

It's a relief to find that the Capri Social Club, lovingly known to the neighbourhood as Irene's, is alive and kicking, and as unfashionable as ever. A true Greenpoint jumble, the back bar, cabinetry, partition and booths, from the lovely old bones of an 1890s saloon, are as splendid as any historic barroom in the city, while the back room is 1950s linoleum tile. For drinks expect only the basics, as befits an Old Man Bar (even though the crowd is younger than it used to be), and in this neighbourhood that means Polish beer and vodka. The jukebox in the rear has the same classic rock and country CDs it did 20 years ago. In NYC there is nothing permanent except change, but we hope Irene's never does.

→ **156 CALYER STREET**

📞 **TEL:** *347 392 7591*

📱 **DAILY:** *4pm-4am*
CASH ONLY

Peter Pan Donut & Pastry Shop

An old reliable in Greenpoint, go expecting a crowd, regardless of the hour. Girls in pink-trimmed green smocks serve a never-ending tsunami of hardcore Peter Pan fans. The doughnuts are excellent, though they tend to be oversized, but we might come here just for the vintage interior. Built-in shelving dating from the shop's 1952 opening displays the doughnuts below hand-lettered price lists. A low, S-shaped counter snakes through the store, surrounded by diner stools. They don't make them like this anymore.

→ 727 MANHATTAN AVENUE

☎ TEL: *718 389 3676*

🖥 MON-FRI: *4.30am-8pm*
SAT: *5am-8pm*
SUN: *5.30am-7pm*
CASH ONLY

Rzeszowska Bakery

It is always a relief to find the Rzeszowska Bakery just the same as our first visit 35 years ago. Your basic concept of doughnuts will be changed forever by their paczki (*"pownch*-kee") the round, fat, Polish version, filled with cherry or prune preserves. You can never be certain what they will be baking on any given day: poppy seed roll, apple strudel, fruit danish, all are possibilities. One thing is for sure, half the neighbourhood will line up on the Saturday before Easter to buy their Sunday babka. But this is nothing like the Jewish babka you may be expecting. The Polish recipe is light, eggy and fluffy, more like a panettone than the dense, sweeter Lower East Side classic. Rejoice that we live in a world with both.

→ **948 MANHATTAN AVENUE**

☎ **TEL:** *718 383 8142*

▯ **DAILY:** *8am-7pm*
CASH ONLY

Bamonte's

Over the course of more than a century, the Bamonte family has made their Italian-American restaurant a Williamsburg landmark. While the bar is generally a pre-dinner meeting spot rather than a destination, it is such a delightful experience that it deserves your full attention. There is no canned music or TV to distract from the pleasures of the room, and you'll enjoy the regulars (who live and breathe Brooklyn no matter where they may have moved on or up to) exchanging greetings in anticipation of another dinner at their favourite restaurant. The familiar faces of the long-time wait staff greet us in the dining room. While the waiters never seem to change, we have noticed the food has become more consistently good over our many visits here. One truth is eternal: order the Pork Chop Alla Bamonte with a mix of sweet peppers if you know what's good for you.

→ **32 WITHERS STREET**

📞 **TEL:** *718 384 8831*

🖥 **MON, WED, THU:** *12noon-10pm*
FRI-SAT: *12noon-11pm*
SUN: *1pm-10pm*

Emily's Pork Store

More than an Italian butcher, a "pork store" makes its own sausages, fresh and dry-cured. Emily's has been at it from 1974. Crammed into this small space, besides the full service butcher counter and sopressata hanging above it, there are cheese, fresh mozzarella and aged imports, and an array of canned products from Italy. Other delicacies fight for floor space: a rack of breads and cookies; a stack of baccalà (dried salt cod); sacks of walnuts, hazelnuts and chestnuts. If this abundance is making you lightheaded you may feel in need of a little snack. Buy a take-out hot dish, baked pasta, maybe meatloaf, or have them make you a sandwich. Ask for an Italian Combo: salami, capicola, mozzarella, oil and vinegar, mixed sweet and hot pickled peppers, on a half loaf of Italian bread. Don't leave without grabbing a bottle of Manhattan Special espresso soda, a neighbourhood staple since 1895, made around the corner on Manhattan Avenue.

→ **426 GRAHAM AVENUE**
TEL: *718 383 7216*

MON: *10am-6.30pm*
TUE-SAT: *8.30am-6.30pm*

Fortunato Brothers Cafe & Pasticceria

The Fortunatos opened their pasticceria in 1976 when this end of Williamsburg was solidly Italian. That this tidy corner business has endured the changing neighbourhood shouldn't be a surprise; everyone loves a good cannoli. Cookies and cakes, and marzipan disguised as figs, cherries, pickles, pizza, and even a feast of seven marzipan fish also do a good trade. If gelato is calling, you might consider a banana split made with three flavors of gelati. The tables by the windows are a great place for an espresso and maybe a Napoleon while you watch the neighbourhood parade.

→ **289 MANHATTAN AVENUE**

📞 **TEL:** *718 387 2281*

📱 **SUN-THU:** *8am-11pm*
   FRI-SAT: *8am-12midnight*

Frost Italian Restaurant

On Frost Street in the far north end of residential Williamsburg, this little restaurant has served Italian-American cuisine since 1959. For an old-fashioned red sauce place they make a remarkably good salad, with a tasty house dressing and pickled mushrooms. Good bread, excellent meatballs, and a very flavorful chicken cacciatore are highlights. Espresso comes to your table with the anisette, gratis, for your caffé corretto.

→ **193 FROST STREET**

📞 TEL: *718 389 3347*

SUN, TUE, WED, THU: *12noon-9.30pm*
FRI: *12noon-12midnight*
SAT: *12noon-10.30pm*
FULL BAR

Gottlieb's Delicatessen

At the edge of the Hasidic part of Williamsburg, Gottlieb's dishes up a pleasing selection of kosher deli fare, with a Hungarian slant. Pastrami, goulash, stuffed cabbage, and where else are you going to go for chulent, the slow-cooked brisket stew? They serve a matzoh ball so light it might be described as fluffy. The small dining area feels like it is still 1962, their first year of business. The line at the take-out counter never ends. Save room for a noodle kugel.

→ 352 ROEBLING STREET

☎ TEL: *718 384 6612*

🍴 SUN-THU: *11.30am-10pm*
   FRI: *11.30am-3pm*

Jr. & Son

This is a 1970s-vintage corner bar with such a low profile we used to think it was never open. Sometimes what you fear to be a dire bucket of blood turns out to be just a bar. Jr. & Son can seem intimidating to strangers, who may assume it is strictly a clubhouse for the natives, but it can be as welcoming a place as any with a little time to warm up. Like most things in life, it helps if you don't make it all about you. Settle in with a couple of beers, show some interest in the old pictures of the local guys and dolls, and you'll find the stories about the old neighbourhood and of Junior and his son come in torrents.

→ 575 LORIMER STREET

☎ TEL: *917 499 3248*

▯ MON-TUE: *11am-7pm*
WED-THU: *11am-12midnight*
FRI: *11am-3am* SAT: *11am-4am*
SUN: *12noon-9pm*
HOURS MAY BE IRREGULAR
CASH ONLY

Peter Luger Steak House

The excitement level is up to 11. Friends gather first at the bar, savour their cocktails while waiting to be seated. The gaslight-era beerhall setting has everyone in a joyous mood, likewise the smell of roasting beef, and the anticipation of dropping a bundle on dinner. You'll order the Porterhouse for two, three or four. And though your seasoned waiter will wrinkle his nose at the suggestions of a salad, go ahead, because you'll also be ordering the the the thick-cut bacon appetiser. When it opened in 1887, the neighbourhood was heavily German and the Williamsburg Bridge, in the shadow of which Luger's sits today, wouldn't be completed for 16 more years. Luger's was purchased by a loyal customer (with an aversion to change, thankfully) in 1950 and has been under the same family management ever since.

> 178 BROADWAY

📞 TEL: *718 387 7400*

🍴 MON-THU: *11.45am-9.45pm*
FRI-SAT: *11.45am-10.45pm*
SUN: *12.45pm-9.45pm*
CASH ONLY (DEBIT CARDS ACCEPTED),
RESERVATIONS ESSENTIAL, FULL BAR.

Sal's Pizzeria

Serving the Italian side of Williamsburg since 1967, this place is always busy with eat-in and take-out trade. Sal's is a neighbourhood institution more than just another slice parlour. Indeed they take their business seriously. Beyond the expected heroes and calzones, the menu extends to pasta entrees and even salads. Many humble pizza joints may boast a big menu, but at Sal's people actually order from it. You'll see great heaps of antipasto, chicken parmigiana, spaghetti and meat-balls, though you should not neglect their excellent pies, with a thin, crisp crust in the classic New York manner. Another rare feature is tap beer: two Italian imports and local favourite Brooklyn Lager. If you see a slice with fried aubergine and mozzarella, by all means pounce.

→ **544 LORIMER STREET**

📞 **TEL:** *718 388 6838*

🍺 **DAILY:** *11am-11pm*
    BEER & WINE

Teddy's

Teddy's claims to be the oldest continually running bar in Brooklyn. More Importantly, we think, they have been an element of continuity in a neighbourhood that seems to change daily. Long gone are the rough working class roots of Williamsburg, and even the bohemian revitalisation, beginning some 30 years ago, has dissipated in a tidal wave of big money and new construction. But Teddy's seems to remain itself, an unpretentious local bar. In 1887 it was a saloon run by an Irishman, later in the 1910s a taproom for the local Peter Doelger Brewery, as the stained glass above the window will testify. Sometime in the 1950s it acquired the name Teddy's. Through the years it has been a dependable social anchor for the Northside and the new owners seem to see their role as caretakers, thankfully. The kitchen is much improved from the old days. Also the interior has been cleaned up a bit, all the better to feast one's eyes on a stellar example of a 19th-century saloon.

→ **96 BERRY STREET**

📞 **TEL:** */18 384 9787*

📱 **MON-THU:** *11am-1am* **FRI-SAT:** *11am-2am* **SUN:** *12noon-6pm*
FULL BAR

DOWNTOWN

Brooklyn Inn

The Brooklyn Inn is, matter-of-factly, a corner bar, but oh, what a corner — 148 Hoyt is an 1850s/1880s Queen Anne beauty. Inside, low lighting enhances the 19th-century charms of dark wood, stained glass, and double-tall ceiling, and there is, blessedly, no television to muck up the mood. The music (jukebox or bartender's iPod) is not too loud. In an age of precious cocktail bars and cookie cutter Irish/sports bars, this is a place with its own personality, and its loyal regulars. Whiskies and craft beers are popular, the bartending is skillful, not flashy. A pool table stands ready in the back room. If your aim is an intimate chat with a friend, some luck may score you the tiny nookery opposite the bar.

→ **148 HOYT STREET**

☎ **TEL:** *718 522 2525*

▯ **MON-THU:** *4pm-4am*
FRI: *3pm-4am*
SAT-SUN: *2pm-4am*
CASH ONLY

Queen Italian Restaurant

The scenery has changed over the years but the feel is still 1950. Call for reservations and you'll be addressed formally, thanked for your business and given an assurance that Franco will greet you upon arrival. The menu is fancy Brooklyn Italian restaurant, but the desserts are unusually inviting; amarena cherries and vanilla gelato doused in espresso, or chocolate ravioli, or fresh dates cooked in spiced wines and served with mascarpone. Fans of the 1970s rock group of the same name may feel their heart skip a beat upon seeing the restaurant's neon sign, which is nearly typeface larceny.

→ 84 COURT STREET
☎ TEL: *718 596 5955*

🍽 MON-THU: *12noon-10pm*
FRI: *12noon-10.30pm*
SAT: *4pm-10.30pm*
SUN: *3pm-10pm*
FULL BAR

Mike's Coffee Shop

Mike's dates from the 1950s when a diner in New York City was called a coffee shop. The whole artisanal coffee craze has muddied the waters, but make no mistake, Mike's is where to be if you want that textbook diner experience. Enormous plates of pancakes or waffles with sausage are popular with students from nearby Pratt Institute trying to maximise their calories for the lowest price.

→ **328 DEKALB AVENUE**
📞 **TEL:** *718 857 1462*

📖 **MON-FRI:** *7am-6pm*
  SAT-SUN: *7am-5pm*
  CASH ONLY

River Café

Most of our Mom and Pop list skews to the affordable (if not downright cheap). Not this one. You will pay plenty at the River Café, but the scenery is included. In 1977 Michael "Buzzy" O'Keeffe turned this decommissioned coffee barge at the foot of the Brooklyn Bridge into a swanky Michelin-starred restaurant. It was the work of a true pioneer to trust people would come to what was then an essentially deserted industrial waterfront. Ironically, now the neighbourhood is flush with money, full of internet start-ups and tech companies, but all staffed with a generation too young to be much interested in the genteel glamour of the River Café. Still, it remains a treat for which New Yorkers will reserve weeks in advance, when they want an extravagant meal with a show-stopping view of Manhattan.

→ 1 WATER STREET

☎ TEL: */18 522 5200*

📖 MON-FRI: *8.30am-11.30am & 5.30pm-11pm*
SAT-SUN: *11.30am-2.30pm & 5.30pm-11pm*
FULL BAR
RESERVATIONS REQUIRED

Frank's Cocktail Lounge

Frank's opened in 1974 and there is without question a cool, swinging '70s vibe to the place: the white stucco merengue ceiling, the red lights, the conversation-pit-style oversized booths, all seem decidedly superfly. It can get loud in the evenings if there is a deejay involved. Early hours are better if jazz or vintage R&B is your trip. Can you dig it?

→ **660 FULTON STREET**
📞 **TEL:** *718 625 9339*

📖 **MON-THU:** *5pm-2am*
  FRI-SAT: *3pm-4am*
  SUN: *3pm-2am*
  CASH ONLY

Fulton Hot Dog King

What could be more perfect to serve the downtown shopping hub known as the Fulton Mall than a corner hot dog stand? How about if they removed the cheesy '70s awning and restored the vintage signage preserved underneath to its 1950 pop! Walking down the block today you can see handsome jumbo letters announcing: FRANKFURTERS just as it looked 60 years ago. The grilled dog is better than average, with a good snap. Optional chilli sauce is the Greek diner classic, with lots of cumin. There are a ridiculous amount of other items available, from burgers to tuna salad to smoothies. Three stools, no pork.

→ 472 FULTON STREET

📞 TEL: *718 858 9799*

📟 DAILY: *7am-8pm*
CASH ONLY

Junior's

Sure, if you like cheesecake, Junior's has the best New York-style out there. It is also a reliably good restaurant in the Jewish deli style. Junior's snappy orange and white striped decor and dependable menu have been Brooklyn favourites since 1950. It is rather spacious which makes it attractive for birthdays and other large parties, so the dining room has a family restaurant feeling. It may surprise new visitors that they also have a proper cocktail lounge. The bar, helmed by Tim, a crackerjack professional, has a devoted crew of regulars, a lot of whom work in the neighbourhood and stop off at the end of the day for attitude adjustment hour. They all seem to be continuing a conversation with each other that started years ago.

→ 386 FLATBUSH AVE EXTENSION

☏ TEL: *718 852 5257*

▯ SUN-THU: *6.30am-12midnight*
FRI-SAT: *6.30am-1am*
FULL BAR

THE WEST

Caputo's Bake Shop

Five generations of Caputos have maintained a bakery on Court Street since opening in 1904. You'll want your bread from Caputo's, but good luck choosing, because there are more options than you could imagine in a shop so small you can barely turn around. Ciabatta and olive bread are favourites, but there's even Irish soda bread and an honourable multi-grain Italian loaf, each sold in a jolly blue and yellow paper sack. After sorting the staples, a little something for your trouble: treat yourself to pie, biscotti, danish, perhaps just some innocent butter cookies.

→ **329 COURT STREET**

☎ **TEL:** *718 875 6871*

⬛ **MON-SAT:** *6am-7pm*
SUN: *6am-5.30pm*
CASH ONLY

D'Amico Coffee Roasters

Three generations of D'Amico have been roasting beans here since 1948. Most of that time at 309 Court Street, though recently the roasting operation was exiled a mile down the road to Red Hook. A wall of bins holds dozens of varieties, blends, dark and light roasts, ground to your specifications by their helpful staff. Or just pop in for a cup and a snack at a table in the back.

→ **309 COURT STREET**

☎ **TEL:** 718 875 5403

▯ **MON-FRI:** 7am-7pm
SAT: 7am-6pm
SUN: 9am-3pm

G. Esposito & Sons Pork Store

Right next door to F. Monteleone, the Espositos have been doing business since 1922. In addition to the expected pork store operation, the butcher counter, Italian sausages and cheeses, they sell a variety of ready-made dishes to carry out. Bakcd ziti and manicotti, meatballs and sauce, rolled eggplant stuffed with ricotta and spinach are among the options. Their prosciutto bread, dense and chewy, riddled with peppery sausage, is a standout.

→ **357 COURT STREET**

☎ **TEL:** *718 875 6863*

🗓 **MON-SAT:** *8am-6pm*
 SUN: *9am-2pm*

Mazzola Bakery

Nicola Mazzola opened his bakery in 1928. In 1980 the torch was passed to the Caravello family. Some will claim their lard bread, with chunks of salami baked inside, is the best in Carroll Gardens, though the Espositos may have something to say about that. The focaccia is very popular. Mornings, the locals mob the place for a fresh cup of coffee and a muffin or roll.

→ 192 **UNION STREET**

☎ TEL: *718 643 1719*

▯ **DAILY:** *6am-8pm*
   CASH ONLY

Monte's

Nothing says 1906 when you walk in the door, but sometimes a family business is less about preserving the past and more concerned with making the changes necessary to survive. Called Angelo's when it opened, in the 1930s it became Monte's Venetian Room, later a favourite hangout for Frank Sinatra and Dean Martin. When Nick Monte died in 2008 the restaurant was in bad shape. The new owners, with roots in the neighbourhood and a connection by marriage to Monte, felt duty-bound to keep what they could and still create a viable business. The name and the old bar are the principal items saved, the big red booths are only inspired by the originals, but some changes are improvements. The menu has clearly been updated for the modern palate, and no one could complain about its quality. The strategy has evidently worked. In an oddball location by the Gowanus Canal, with no foot traffic to speak of, Monte's is a thriving little neighbourhood joint again.

→ 451 CARROLL STREET

☎ TEL: *718 852 7800*

▤ TUE-THU: *5pm-10pm* FRI: *5pm-11pm* SAT: *10am-11pm* SUN: *10am-10pm*
FULL BAR

F. Monteleone Bakery

This sweet Italian bakery and pastry shop is the wedding of two revered Brooklyn bakeries, Monteleone and Cammerari. Cammerari's bread shop opened up the street in 1921. In 2007, to the delight of Carroll Gardens customers, they merged with the pastry wizards at Monteleone. The shop dates from 1904 and it maintains an old-time appeal that's hard to beat. Cookies, pastries and cakes abound, choosing will be a difficult task. There are a couple of small tables in the back, if you can't wait for home, and there's coffee to wash down your haul.

→ 355 COURT STREET

☎ TEL: /18 852 5600

▯ DAILY: 8am-9pm

Damascus Bakery

Damascus has been baking pita bread in downtown Brooklyn since 1930. The physical plant is now in DUMBO, but their retail store on Atlantic Avenue remains the place for Syrian pastries and other Middle Eastern baked goods: breads with sesame seeds or zahtar, honeyed baklava, date cookies, strudels and great cylinders of halvah. Setting aside dessert for a moment, you will also discover imported canned and frozen delicacies, dried fruits, and some prepared dishes such as stuffed grape leaves and bean salads.

→ 195 ATLANTIC AVENUE

📞 TEL: *718 625 7070*

📱 DAILY: *7am-8pm*

Long Island Bar

Opened in the 1950s as a restaurant serving hungry longshoremen off the docks at the end of the avenue, the Long Island stood shuttered for years awaiting its rebirth as a fashionable cocktail bar and restaurant. Thankfully no major changes were made to the interior, everything has just been buffed up to a gloss; the booths, the Formica walls, even the myriad cigarette burns in the woodwork have been preserved, and the result is a handsome time capsule. As the clientele— and their tastes—have changed, so of course will the menu. Expect a polished cocktail and some sophisticated bar food.

→ **110 ATLANTIC AVENUE**

📞 **TEL:** *718 625 8908*

🍴 **SUN-THU:** *5.30pm-12midnight*
FRI-SAT: *5.30pm-2am*

Montero Bar & Grill

The chaotic jumble of nautical curiosities covering the interior testify to Montero's early days as the choice for workers off the nearby piers and sailors finding themselves beached on Atlantic Avenue. This has been a neighbourhood stalwart since 1947. The grill is long gone and the bar is best for shot-and-a-beer basics, although you can get a standard cocktail without complaint. It is still a family business, as welcoming and without pretension as a visit to a favourite uncle, and with as many stories to tell.

→ **73 ATLANTIC AVENUE**

📞 **TEL:** *646 729 4129*

🔖 **DAILY:** *2pm-4am*

Oriental Pastry and Grocery

Looking for dried lemons or limes? Need to choose from three types of golden raisins and welcome an opinion on the Yemeni ones? You're in the right place. This spice and grocery store has been the Moustapha family business since 1967. Don't let the intimacy of this shop scare you off, they're helpful and friendly. This is the place you want to go to have a conversation instead of fighting a crowd of foodies for a spot at the olive bar at the organic superstore. The cupboards and cases and bins and jars are chockablock with dried fruits, loose herbal teas, olives galore, pickled vegetables, baklava, packaged cookies and other sweets, all at encouraging prices. This is classic Atlantic Avenue.

→ 170 ATLANTIC AVENUE

📞 TEL: *718 875 7687*

🗓 DAILY: *10am-8.30pm*

Sahadi's

A cornerstone of the Syrian and Lebanese communities in Brooklyn, Sahadi's opened on Atlantic Avenue in 1948 selling Middle Eastern imports. They have expanded over the years, and today you'll find more European products than before, and local NY state specialty items in addition to the plethora of dried fruits, nuts, coffee, candy, cheeses, meats. A massive Trader Joe's gourmet supermarket has opened up the street, but Sahadi's business didn't seem to be suffering on a recent Saturday, a testament to the loyalty of their long-time customers.

→ 187 ATLANTIC AVENUE
📞 TEL: *718 624 4550*

📱 MON-SAT: *9am-7pm*

Sam's Restaurant

Despite the sign out front, no one goes here for steaks and chops, the pizza is the draw, though the kitchen renders quite good examples of the classic red sauce pasta dishes, too. Sam's has been here since 1930, and your waiter, Louis, about half of that. They own the building, so no one worries about the lack of a crowd, or how quick they get around to taking your order, either. More time for you to soak up the aging allure of the red vinyl booths, checked tablecloth, wood paneled dining room. From the menu: "If your wife can't cook, don't divorce her, keep her and eat at Sam's... you'll both be happy." Well, even if you both cook, an evening here is always tops.

→ **238 COURT STREET**

📞 **TEL:** *718 596 3458*

🗓 **WED-MON:** *12noon-10pm*
  CASH ONLY
  FULL BAR

Antonio's Pizzeria

Their 1950 pedigree is evident with a first glance at the spectacular neon sign on the Flatbush storefront. Besides the usual New York-style and Sicilian slices, Antonio's has a fine example of the "Grandma slice," the current rage sweeping Brooklyn pizzerias. A relatively recent innovation imported from Long Island, the Grandma is a square slice with a thin, homestyle crust, light on the cheese and heavy on the sauce. At Antonio's it is herbal and fresh tasting. Plus you get a bonus comedy moment when your slice hits the counter and the call goes out, "Grandma!" to which you sheepishly answer, "Here."

→ **318 FLATBUSH AVENUE**

☎ **TEL:** *718 398 2300*

▯ **SUN-THU:** *11am-11pm*
   FRI-SAT: *11am-12midnight*

Smith's Tavern

Around the turn of this century the folks at Smith's had the idea to redo the interior of their 1931-vintage barroom. They did quite an eye-popping job of it, installing faux stone arches and a bizarre vaulted wood ceiling. A few elements escaped ruination: the lovely old bar itself, a bit of stained glass. Despite efforts to update the place it's still a blue collar island in a sea of bros and woo-girls, and for that we are grateful. A jukebox can be a major part in defining a bar's character. Sadly, the old one has been replaced with the usual satellite gizmo, but recently our night was saved by an older gent who dominated the machine with a tasty selection of '70s soul.

→ **440 5TH AVENUE**
☎ **TEL:** *718 788 5218*

▯ **MON-SAT:** *8am-4am*
   SUN: *12noon-4am*
   CASH ONLY

Two Toms

Two Toms has been a neighbourhood fixture since 1948, and it is the essence of a Mom and Pop joint. It all happens in a room so bare it seems like an empty stage waiting for a show. The curtain goes up when the staff and a cast of special guest stars — their customers — begin a dialogue on what dinner will be this evening. Everything at Two Toms is a negotiation — what are you hungry for? Giant ribeye steaks and double thick pork chops are two best sellers. But you gotta have the baked clams, right? The long, boxcar-shaped room attracts large parties, which can get loud, but that is when the Two Toms show is the most entertaining.

→ **255 THIRD AVENUE**

📞 **TEL:** *718 875 8689*

📱 **TUE-SAT:** *5pm-10pm*
   BEER & WINE

Defonte's Sandwich Shop

Have you seen grown men looking into a deli case with the anticipation of a five-year-old at the candy counter? If not, come to Defonte's. Business is brisk, despite the location in an industrial section of Red Hook that is severely isolated by a highway exchange, a reminder of how cruelly neighbourhoods can be surgically altered by city planners. Defonte's brings in a steady stream of locals — residents and labourers — plus devotees from all over via automobile. To get here on foot is a small trek, but worthwhile. The small storefront evolved from a hangout for dock workers in 1922 to the busy operation it is today. Countless combos are available, but the hot sandwiches are king. Meatballs, certainly, or go for pork with broccoli rabe, homemade mozzarella and eggplant, or maybe a peppers and egg hero. No tables or chairs, so mostly takeout, or wolf it down standing at the short counter by the entrance.

→ **379 COLUMBIA STREET**

📞 **TEL:** *718 625 8052*

🔲 **MON-SAT:** *10am-5pm*

Ferdinando's Focacceria

This revered old doll of a restaurant has served a menu of now-rare Palermo cookery since 1904. The original tile floors and tin ceiling are an appropriate backdrop for such nearly forgotten antique delicacies as vastedda, a sandwich of calf's spleen and ricotta on a roll. No, really, it's delicious. If offal makes you squeamish, try another Sicilian specialty, pasta con sarde, with sardines, fennel and currants. The menu is small, a good sign by our lights, indicating they concentrate on what they do best. Speaking of which, yes, you will be filling up on focaccia bread even before your pasta and sandwich arrive, there's no way to resist.

→ 151 UNION STREET

☎ TEL: *718 855 1545*

🕐 MON-THU: *11am-8pm* FRI-SAT: *11am-10pm*
CREDIT CARDS ON WEEKENDS ONLY, MINIMUM $20
BEER & WINE

Sunny's Bar

The jumble shop charms of Sunny's will be familiar to any true connoisseur of old New York bars. It is as famous a dive as any, certainly more popular today than ever. Luckily for fans, the trip out to the very edge of Red Hook is arduous enough to keep away casual look-ie-lous. It's hard to describe the quirky character of Sunny's, although recently dozens have tried in print. It is part low-down waterfront bucket-of-blood, part artists' bar, like a Last Exit To Brooklyn version of Max's Kansas City. Locals and tourists mix with no apparent friction. Next up on the turntable behind the bar, the bartender picks another '60s soul album out of the pile. If any of that appeals to you, you should make the journey.

→ **253 CONOVER STREET**

📞 **TEL:** *718 625 8211*

📱 **MON-TUE:** *4pm-2am*
WED-FRI: *4pm-4am*
SAT: *11am-4am*
SUN: *11am-12midnight*
CASH ONLY

Danish Athletic Club

A century ago, this area, where Bay Ridge and Sunset Park meet, was the hub of a Scandinavian community in Brooklyn. The Danish Athletic Club was founded in 1892, and has been at this address since the 1940s. A few doors down 65th Street is the Swedish Football Club, and the Norwegians are represented by the Sporting Club Gjøa, around the corner on 62nd Street (both private). The Danish Athletic Club has a wonderful old bar that is generously open to non-members. Order an aquavit (discussions of national varieties may ensue) and pump some money into one of the last jukeboxes in town that plays genuine 45rpm records. Then retire to the dining room, which claims to be the oldest continuously running restaurant in Bay Ridge, for a satisfyingly old-fashioned Scandinavian dinner at an embarrassingly low price.

→ 735-741 65TH STREET

☎ TEL. *718 748 7844*

▯ WED-SAT: *5pm-8pm*
SUN: *2pm-7pm*
(always a good idea to call first)

International Restaurant

Sunset Park was long home to Irish, Italian and Scandinavian immigrants. Hispanic and Chinese Americans now comprise the majority. The International Restaurant has served Dominican food since 1984. It is a cheery diner, dishing up breakfast, lunch and dinner to a steady stream of locals hungry for Caribbean dishes. A sancocho, meat stewed with yuca and plantain, is a daily special. Roast pork sandwiches are popular as are asopao, bowls of "soupy rice" with chicken or seafood. A good accompaniment to pork chops or pernil is rice and pigeon peas. Come early for Dominican breakfast specials, featuring fried cheese or spicy salchipon; stay late for Piña Coladas or Margaritas.

→ **4408 5TH AVENUE**

📞 **TEL:** *718 438 2009*

▯ **DAILY:** *7am-12midnight*
FULL BAR

Irish Haven Bar

Inside this corner bar it is 1964 preserved in aspic. This is an Irish bar that is Brooklyn as it used to be, none of your queasy pub-in-a-box generic tat currently the trend. Another welcome rarity, they manage to serve a pint of Guinness at a proper temperature. A real juke-box always establishes character and, although this one is CD-fueled, it sets the evening's mood from Sinatra to Blondie and, of course, a smattering of the Pogues.

→ **5721 4TH AVENUE**

TEL: *718 439 9893*

MON-SAT: *8am-4am*
SUN: *12noon-4am*

Johnny's Pizza

Sunset Park's favourite slice since 1968. Cosy. The plain slice is excellent, as is a lasagna slice, dots of meat sauce alternating with blobs of ricotta. They make a tiny sandwich from a garlic knot, halved and filled with ham and cheese. A few years ago a huge pizza franchise with a terrible product and a similar name, Papa John's, planned to open a store next door to Johnny's. The resulting outrage in the neighbourhood, culminating in a petition and a picket line, persuaded them to try elsewhere. The corporate villain exits the stage to a chorus of hisses and catcalls.

→ 5806 5TH AVENUE
☎ TEL: *718 492 9735*

▯ MON–WED: *11.30am-9pm*
   THU–SAT: *11.30am-10pm*
   SUN: *12 noon-9pm*

Melody Lanes

Williamsburg has two bowling-themed bars, but sometimes we want to roll a few frames in a hipster-free environment. Bowlers in Sunset Park have done that at Melody Lanes since 1960, all without a trace of irony. It can be thirsty work. Fortunately, there is a bar. It is presided over by one of the most iconoclastic native Brooklynites you may ever meet, Peter Napolitano, resplendent in starched shirt front and snow-white rocker mutton chops. His job may be tending bar, but his vocation is philosophy, his lifelong project in this vein is a universal explanation, or as he calls it, an "every-think" theory and rest assured, he will share it with you. Every shift is really a seminar and tuition is the price of a drink.

→ **461 37TH STREET**

☎ **TEL:** *718 832 2695*

🏠 **SUN-THU:** *6pm-12midnight*
  FRI-SAT: *6pm-2am (but call if it's late)*

CENTRAL
BROOKLYN

D. Coluccio & Sons

Importers of Italian products since 1964, selling many items exclusive to Coluccio in this country. Southern Italy is their specialty, and you'll find out-of-the-ordinary foodstuffs such as Sicilian *pomodoro di paccino* — cherry tomatoes — dried or canned, and quite a few varieties of bitter chinotto sodas. If packaging is to you an art form, this is your place. There are licorice lozenges worth picking up if just for their handsome pillbox-sized tins, candy boxes of jordan almonds that could be props from a 1950s wedding scene, and a whole wall of beautiful dried pastas sold in eye-pleasing cardboard boxes. At the meat, cheese and olive counter offering salamis, sweet or hot, some made with boar, you may hear more Italian conversation between customer and counterman than probably anywhere in the New World.

→ **1214 60TH STREET**

☎ **TEL:** *718 436 6700*

▯ **MON-SAT:** *8am-6pm*
SUN: *8am-2pm*

Colandrea New Corner

It's a hike from the train, but so worth it. Opened in 1936, with some renovations in the disco '70s as evident from the eye-popping artwork on the walls, exposed brick interior and the rec room paneling in the bar. People that grew up with the New Corner want it to stay the pleasantly old-fashioned dependable Brooklyn Italian-American red sauce hangout that it is, and the third generation Colandreas do their best to oblige. On Feel Good Thursdays the fortunate are serenaded by accordion music. Quick Draw lottery screens hang in the bar and dining rooms. If you don't like to gamble, order the cacciatore, it's always a sure thing. But you won't go wrong with lasagna or manicotti, or the pork chops, served with potato croquettes.

→ 7201 EIGHTH AVENUE

📞 TEL: *718 833 0800*

🍽 MON-THU: *12noon-10pm*
FRI-SAT: *12noon-11pm*
SUN: *12noon-9.30pm*
FULL BAR

Nicoletti Coffee

No fancy frou-frou $9 beverages, no cranberry scones, no wifi. A handwritten sign in the door warns that Nicoletti will not sell you a cup of a coffee. However — if you play your cards right, in a short while you may be sipping an excellent espresso as you hobnob with the loquacious Nicoletti. Rule one is you do not ask. Coffee is offered on Nicoletti's terms exclusively, a single shot, and on the house. One poor soul once asked for a double espresso and was told the machine was broken. The interior features a sleeping dog and collection of broken down chairs pointed at a large television so Nicoletti can relax with the latest football match between customers. The walls are lined with an astounding variety of stovetop espresso pots. Does anyone buy them? Whole beans or ground, the coffee is fresh from the roaster and cheap. Since 1972.

→ **6723 13TH AVENUE**

☎ **TEL:** *718 232 2259*

▯ **MON-SAT:** *10am-6pm*

Soccer Tavern

Back in the 1930s it was Kerr's Restaurant And Bar,
but it has been the Soccer Tavern since the 1950s. It's
the last Irish bar standing in the borough's newest
and fastest growing Chinatown. True to the name,
they indeed love their football here. The rear of the
bar is dominated by screenings of the current match.
A dart board is on the wall, as well as team trophies.
Another shelf holds the barroom staple (see Sunny's,
Homestretch) chalkware figurines of old movie stars:
Gable, WC Fields, Laurel & Hardy, and… some lumi-
nary we can't identify. That's something to talk about
while drinking. A floor of linoleum squares and a drop
panel ceiling make the small room resemble a finished
basement rumpus room, but a careful look around will
reveal a worn but still lovely old bar top and back bar,
dating from the 1930s, one suspects.

→ **6004 8TH AVENUE**

☎ **TEL:** *718 439 9336*

▯ **DAILY:** *9am-3am*
   CASH ONLY

Denny's Steak Pub

Don't go to Denny's for steak, because the kitchen is long gone. On a cold Saturday afternoon we scored a pretty good hot dog, a snack offered free to customers, but that's the most food you can hope for. According to legend, the original Denny's was in Park Slope but this incarnation has squatted above the Church Avenue F station since 1959. It's a neighbourhood bar with a lively multigenerational scene, serving good tap beer, including local favourite Brooklyn Lager, and there's nothing fancy in the realm of drinks, just the basics competently delivered. For the athletic, there is a pool table. The latest upgrade to the interior was apparently in the 1970s, judging from the rec-room-on-the-skids ambiance; the brick arches and trim might have been found in the Brady Bunch basement. The backlit grid above the bar casts a jolly red plastic glow that makes bartender and patrons look like so many bags of french fries under a heat lamp. And then there is that ceiling fan. At some point the ceiling was lowered to be level with the fan blades. Whatever the reason, this built-in quality feels vaguely menacing, like a set from Terry Gilliam's *Brazil*.

→ **106 BEVERLEY ROAD**

☏ **TEL:** *718 435 2156*

▯ **MON-THU:** *9am-4am* **FRI-SAT:** *9am-2am* **SUN:** *9am-12noon*

Chiffon Kosher Cake Center

Here is the inspiring tale of a long running family business rescued and reborn, and, like an old movie cliffhanger, just in the nick of time, too. The original Chiffon's Kosher Bakery began in 1960, providing an array of sweets, cookies and pastries, and savoury rye breads to their Jewish neighbours in Midwood. After 40-odd years the owners wanted to sell and luckily found capable buyers who had learned their trade at Gertel's, the legendary bakery which at that moment was ending its reign on Grand Street on the Lower East Side. Go for the marble sponge cake, but don't miss the 1960s Howard Johnson's clock on the wall.

→ **430 AVENUE P**

📞 **TEL:** *718 998 7530*

📱 **SUN-WED:** *5am-7pm*
   THU: *5am-9pm*
   FRI: *5am-3pm*
   CLOSED SAT

Di Fara Pizza

The most famous pizzeria in Brooklyn is Di Fara. Presided over by master pizzaiolo Domenico De Marco, serious pizza fanatics must make a pilgrimage to this Midwood store, like a mozzarella hajj. If pizza is the reason you get up in the morning, you know all of that. If it isn't? Then keep these suggestions in mind before you make your first visit: wear comfortable shoes, make sure your phone has a full charge, do a little meditation to calm your thoughts, be prepared to wait. Patience, novice, pizza nirvana cannot be attained without some sacrifice.

→ 1424 AVENUE J

📞 TEL: *718 258 1367*

📱 TUE-SAT: *12noon-8pm*
   SUN: *1pm-8pm*

JoMart Chocolates

This unassuming shop is a comfortable fit between old-timey and the modern world. JoMart's hand-dipped chocolates range from the classic — nut clusters, nonpareils — to chic and contemporary — ganache-stuffed figs, marshmallows (recommended by the New York Times for adding to hot cocoa) and truffles. The more you look, the more and more and more varieties you need. Beyond the main candyland you'll find an additional storefront for baking and candy-making supplies, and a discreet peek to the back will get you an eyeful of where the magic happens. Owner Michael Rogak uses the same copper kettles and stove as his father Martin and cousin Joe did for fashioning sweets back in 1946. While you're there, nab a set of chocolate handcuffs for your favourite police officer.

→ **2917 AVENUE R**

☎ **TEL:** *718 375 1277*

▯ **MON-SAT:** *9am-6.30pm*

Taci's Beyti

In a predominantly Orthodox Jewish neighbourhood in Midwood you can find this busy Turkish restaurant. Opened in 1988, Taci's serves all your favourites: kebabs, whole grilled fish and lamb chops. Their adana kebab served over pide bread drenched in hot yogurt is a standout. And about that bread, it is superb, fresh baked with toasted nigella (black sesame) seeds. For our money, the Turks make the best stuffed grape leaves going, and those at Taci's are a hit; super homemade, the rice redolent of cinnamon, with currants and pine nuts. Portions are large, and sharing is the way to go. They serve no alcohol, you must bring your own, but there are two liquor stores on the block.

→ **1953-1955 CONEY ISLAND AVENUE**

📞 **TEL:** *718 627 5750*

▯ **DAILY:** *12noon-11pm*
BYOB

Allan's Bakery

The Jamaican community in Brooklyn has looked to Allan's Bakery for a taste of home since 1961. Folks come from all around for dense and slightly sweet "hardo" bread and rolls, coconut bake and cassava pone. Patties of beef, chicken or codfish are also popular. For special occasions there are rum-rich and fruity black cake, sponge cakes, red velvet cake and cross buns during the holiday season. The high quality of their baked goods is no secret, so be prepared for long lines on a weekend.

> 1109 NOSTRAND AVENUE

📞 TEL: *718 744 7892*

🖥 TUE-FRI: *7.30am-7pm*
  SAT: *7.30am-7.30pm*
  SUN: *7.30am-5.30pm*

Mitchell's Soul Food

Any aficionado of Southern cooking will know at first sniff they have hit gold when they walk in this plain, but cosy, Prospect Heights storefront. Wear your eating trousers, you are in for a substantial meal. The fried fish is exceptional: indeed, it was Mitchell's main product some years back, but we are thrilled they have expanded their menu to a full soul food feast. Unbeatable fried chicken, barbecued ribs, okra and tomatoes, sugary yams, collard greens and cornbread — you want it, they got it. More than 40 years on the block, they have witnessed the neighbourhood slowly gentrify. Whatever changes may come, here's hoping there will always be room for the real deal, like Mitchell's. The apartment-like kitchen and welcoming informality makes a visit seem more like a trip home than a restaurant.

→ **617 VANDERBILT AVENUE**

📞 **TEL:** *718 789 3212*

📱 **WED-THU:** *12noon-9.30pm* **FRI-SAT:** *12noon-10.30pm* **SUN:** *1pm-8pm*
  BEER & WINE
  CASH ONLY

Tom's Restaurant

This diner a few blocks from the Brooklyn Museum has seen the neighbourhood's ups and downs in its 80 years, and become a destination for breakfast and lunch. Today it looks more '70s hippie than '30s diner; mismatched mugs rather than restaurant china. It has that lived-in look. The breakfast menu goes from basics to pumpkin pancakes and other gooey delights. Lunch is sandwiches, quesadillas, burgers and meat and potato plates. The vegetables can be surprisingly good, as is their oddly pleasing garlic bread of split hamburger buns with garlic and margarine. Can't say the same for freezer bag fries with the superstarch coating. A little pricey for what it is, but the friendly service and cherry lime rickeys make up for it.

> 782 WASHINGTON AVENUE

☎ TEL: *718 636 9738*

▯ MON-SAT: *7am-4pm*
  SUN: *8am-4pm*
  CASH ONLY

Farrell's Bar & Grill

Farrell's is a 1933-vintage holdover from when this area, Windsor Terrace, could be described in two words: Irish and tough. The crowd here is, as it has always been, primarily police and firemen, active and retired, and starting about 4pm the place fills with construction workers. Women are still something of a novelty. You'll find no corporate beer promos or phony nostalgia on the walls, and not even a stool to detract from the simple beauty of the long mahogany bar. A small draft comes in a graceful seven ounce pony glass, but order a large and you will get an ugly 32 oz. Styrofoam cup, a Farrell's innovation that lets you take your drink outside to have smoke, thus dodging the prohibition on public drinking. That's the theory anyway, but it would be a friendless cop indeed who gave out tickets at Farrell's.

→ **215 PROSPECT PARK WEST**

☏ **TEL:** *718 788 8779*

▯ **MON-SAT:** *10am-4am*
SUN: *12noon-4am*

Anopoli Ice Cream Parlor

Once a staple of the restaurant biz, ice cream parlours are now rare, sadly, but rare is an apt word for Anopoli, which first opened its doors in 1897. On the walls, photos from the 1920s testify how little it has changed over the decades, and that is how the neighbourhood clientele like it. Brass lighting fixtures, tile floors and cosy booths, a line of stools at the counter in front, make an effective time machine. Anopoli still makes ice cream with old-time flavours like maple walnut and butter pecan, and it's one of the last places in town to get a decent malted milkshake. Anapoli is more than just sweet stuff; they offer a full diner menu. For lunch try an egg salad sandwich with bacon, a perfect combo that had somehow previously eluded us.

→ **6920 3RD AVENUE**

☎ **TEL:** *718 748 3863*

▯ **SUN-THU:** *7am-7.30pm*
  FRI-SAT: *7am-9pm*

Espresso Pizza

The textbook definition of a Brooklyn pizza shop would look very much like Espresso Pizza in Bensonhurst. No quirks, nothing fancy, but something close to perfect in its humble lack of personality. The red enamel storefront, the no nonsense menu, even its close proximity to the subway, add up to everything you want from a pizzeria. Similarly, the slice is a nearly perfect balance of the elements: thin crust, neither too much nor to little cheese, marinara sauce with a hint of sweetness. They have been at it since the 1970s. Satisfying, just like you pictured it.

→ **9403 5TH AVENUE**

📞 **TEL:** *718 833 8750*

🍴 **MON-SAT:** *11am-10pm*
   SUN: *12noon-9pm*

Kelly's Tavern

It always feels like 3am in great bars like Kelly's. Full or empty, summer or winter, 1932 or today, it's a refuge. Time flies. Or stands still. The ponies are running on the TVs but conversation is still king, barring those moments when the "classic" rock from the pernicious iCloud jukebox promotes a singalong. A 1940s cigarette machine, presumably non-working, hibernates near the alternate Fifth Avenue entrance. The short beer glass is still popular for the bottled beer drinker at Kelly's. Behind the bar, between the cash registers, is a framed tribute to "H Block Martyrs." Pro-IRA sentiment is not that uncommon in a NYC Irish bar, of course, but it is not always so overt. The regulars are a friendly lot, eager to pry a fresh story out of a newcomer.

→ **9259 4TH AVENUE**

📞 **TEL:** *718 491-1707*

🍺 **MON-SAT:** *11am-4am*
　　SUN: *12noon–4am*

Leske's Bakery

A holdover from the days when Bay Ridge was home to a large Scandinavian community, Leske's opened in 1961. It closed in 2011, but happily it was quickly reconstituted, re-hiring the same bakers. That means you can once again get their excellent danish pastries, including a pretzel-shaped kringler, Swedish limpa bread, gingerbread cookies, apple strudels, and an enormous assortment of other favourites, plus old-time New York classics like black and white cookies, jelly doughnuts, Brooklyn blackout cake and cheesecakes.

→ **7612 5TH AVENUE**

☎ **TEL:** *718 680 2323*

🖥 **DAILY:** *5am-8pm*

Mike's Donut Shop

Mike's has been Bay Ridge's favourite doughnut since 1976. Down the block squats an outlet of their major corporate franchise competition, like a cat staring at a mouse hole, waiting to wipe them out. The crew at Mike's doesn't seem worried. They bake a superior product. A row of stools at a counter, a few tables on the side, fresh doughnuts, hot coffee and an energetic counterman to sell them. This has been the winning formula for 40 years.

→ **6822 5TH AVENUE**

📞 **TEL:** *718 745 6980*

📱 **MON-FRI:** *6am-6pm*

Nino's Pizza

Along with great pizza (regular slice, Sicilian and their "Gran Ma Ma" — how Addams Family!), the stromboli roll slices and rice balls are big sellers here. There is no finer a recommendation than an excited tween with braces giving you an unsolicited testimonial on the riceball: "You gotta get one of these with meat and peas, and you gotta eat them with sauce." We also partook of Nino's innovative take on the garlic knot; little $1 snack sandwiches with a slice each of pepperoni and mozzarella on garlic bread. Decor at Nino's is something above average, meaning they seem to have actually thought about it. Vintage wooden pizza peels adorn the walls. Since 1978.

→ **9110 3RD AVENUE**
☎ **TEL:** *718 680 0222*

▯ **DAILY:** *10am-11pm*

O'Sullivan's Bar and Grill

Family owned and operated since 1934, O'Sullivan's is the place to catch up on neighbourhood scuttlebutt. The regulars reign here in the late afternoon, as a steady stream of customers pop in for an after-work pint. The dining room in back is especially popular on weekends for brunch. Don't come here expecting the 1930s, the decor is stuck in what appears to be a '70s remodel, but the spirit of old Bay Ridge makes it worth your time.

→ 8902 3RD AVENUE

☏ TEL: *718 745 9619*

▯ DAILY: *8am-2am*
KITCHEN: *5pm-10pm*
SUNDAY BRUNCH: *12noon-3pm*
CASH ONLY

Plaka Taverna

On this busy crossroads since 1980, tiny Plaka Taverna serves Greek home-style cooking. From the outside it may look like an inhospitable greasy spoon, but step inside and the waitress is calling you her "darlink" before you get your coat off. Grilled meats are excellent, with special commendation going to the loukaniko, fennel pork sausage. A carafe of wine comes in a taverna traditional copper pitcher with small rocks glasses. Nothing here is fancier than what your grandmother cooks, but it tastes like Greek soul food. Horta, a plate of braised dandelion greens with a squeeze of lemon and a bit of salt, couldn't be more down-home, or more pleasing.

→ **406 86TH STREET**
☎ **TEL:** *718 680 3056*

▯ **SUN-THU:** *11am-10pm*
FRI-SAT: *11am-11pm*
BEER & WINE
CASH ONLY

Royal Restaurant

There has been a Royal Restaurant at this address since the 1940s, but this incarnation's well-preserved interior dates from 1981. This is a lovely example of a diner, with twin U-shaped counters reminiscent of a Chock Full o' Nuts in miniature. A row of booths, the dark wood grain panelling and burnt orange upholstery furnishes a warm atmosphere. The food is, as expected, nothing fancy, but dependably satisfying.

→ **7609 5TH AVENUE**

☎ **TEL:** *718 745 3444*

▯ **MON-SAT:** *6am-8pm*
   SUN: *7am-5pm*

Sancho's

Once upon a time, there was a genre of Spanish restaurant, somewhat formal, white tablecloths and red jackets, lots of lobsters and paella and inexpensive red wine. Greenwich Village and Chelsea was where you found most of them, and recently they have been dropping like flies. As fans of this dying breed, we were delighted to find Sancho's in Bay Ridge. Though comparatively young at 33 years of age, it is a throwback to those old-fashioned Spanish places in the Village. The menu is typical of the genre, with an emphasis on specialities of Valencia.

> 7410 3RD AVENUE

📞 TEL: *718 748 0770*

🍴 SUN, MON, WED, THU: *12noon-10pm*
FRI-SAT: *12noon-11pm*
FULL BAR

Skinflints

A tavern called Skinflints just has to be a product of
the 1970s fashion for Gay '90s-themed restaurants.
Expecting to find another P.J. Clarke's knock-off
rendered in Formica and vinyl, imagine our surprise to
find the well preserved remnants of an Edwardian ice
cream parlour dating from 1915. Mahogany cabinetry,
marble counter front, brass lighting fixtures and leaded
stained glass abound. A stained glass sign above the
entrance to the dining room reads Meyer & Blohm, the
ice cream and candy store in this space which mirac-
ulously lasted through the 1960s. Skinflints began in
1975, and the prevailing taste for old-timey bars must
have helped the decision to keep renovations to a minimum. They became famous for serving a hamburger
on what we in the States call an English muffin — the
height of sophistication in the '70s — which they
continue to this day.

→ **7902 5TH AVENUE**

☎ **TEL:** *718 745 1116*

▯ **MON-THU:** *11.30am-1am* **FRI-SAT:** *11.30am-3am*
　SUN: *12noon-12midnight*
　FULL BAR

Three Jolly Pigeons

When the trendy becomes oppressive nothing satisfies like a good old-time saloon. There has been a bar on this site, Prohibition notwithstanding, since at least 1907. Now called Three Jolly Pigeons, it is as no-nonsense blue-collar as the neighbourhood. Do not even think about grandiose mixology, it's nothing but the basics here. And yet... the green and white tile floors, tin ceiling, wood partition and the stained-glass kiosk over the gents' (just like one much-revered at P.J. Clarke's) are reminders of the elegant past, and ample reasons for a visit.

→ **6802 THIRD AVENUE**

☎ **TEL:** *718 745 9350*

▯ **MON-SAT:** *10am-4am*
  SUN: *12noon-4am*

Homestretch Bar

Come for the cheap drinks and stay for the sensational horse racing mural, dated 1979. This is quintessential hometown Bensonhurst, straight out of Central Casting, from the young and old local patrons to the personable bartender with her jet-black bob that looks like it might date from the 1970 opening of the place. Beneath the cheerful collection of beer promos and miscellaneous decoration (those chalkware movie stars, again) that has accumulated over the decades, is a lovely handmade back bar, the likes of which has become all too rare lately.

→ **214 KINGS HIGHWAY**
☎ **TEL:** *718 372 9719*

▯ **THU-SAT:** *10am-4am*
  SUN-MON: *10am-2am*
  TUE-WED: *10am-3am*
  CASH ONLY

Il Fornaretto

This no-frills shop is truly a window back to the days when just a small counter would front the workshop. In contrast to the numerous NYC Italian bakeries with a bewildering display of sweets, Il Fornaretto, *the little baker*, narrows it down to bread. Or breads. There are semolina, focaccia, spacatella and toscano, some dotted with olive or prosciutto, plus six varieties of taralli, those o-shaped crackers that are a snappy addition to any cocktail hour. Well, there's anisette biscotti and vanilla cookies, too, for your coffee. Established 1927, in Manhattan's Little Italy, they decamped for the wilds of Bensonhurst and an existing coal oven bakery some years later.

→ **7616 17TH AVENUE**

✆ **TEL:** *718 236 6669*

▯ **MON-SAT:** *8am-7pm*
  SUN: *8am-4pm*

J&V Pizzeria

"The Home of the "Jo Jo"" proclaims the awning above this idiosyncratic pizzeria dating from 1950. No menu posted on the walls, nor in a takeout sheet, so just look in the case and choose. The Jo-Jo, we learned, is a meatball or chicken parm on garlic bread. This wasn't their only innovation, legend has it they were also the first in Brooklyn to sell pizza by the slice. Well, maybe. J&V's entry in the grandma slice competition is excellent — tasting of tomato and olive oil. The wood-paneled walls, stone mosaic floor and plastic booth seating give the interior a 1970s look.

→ **6322 18TH AVENUE**

📞 **TEL:** *718 232 2700*

🖥 **DAILY:** *11am-12midnight*

John's Deli

John's has been the place to go for sandwiches in Bensonhurst since 1968. Their flagship is a mound of thin-sliced rare roast beef, mozzarella, braised onions and brown gravy on a hero. The cognoscenti will order extra gravy on the side for dipping. Other hot hero favourites are the meatball marinara, veal cutlet and, on weekends, a fried shrimp sandwich. A multitude of cold cut combos are available too. Some folks swear by their breaded, deep fried ravioli, but do not brag about that to your cardiologist. Don't be put off by the crowds during the lunch rush, the turnover will be quicker than you expect.

→ 2033 STILLWELL AVENUE

☎ TEL: *718 372 7481*

▯ MON-SAT: *8am-10pm*
SUN: *8am-9pm*

La Palina

This being Bensonhurst, there is no Brooklyn stereotype too broad. On a recent visit the music burbled on at a volume low enough to barely graze our consciousness, so we only gradually became aware we were listening to the Bee Gees' *Stayin' Alive*. Because what else you gonna play to follow Johnny Maestro? The original La Palina opened in 1930 downtown on Navy Street, now buried under a freeway, the current location dates from 1955. The vaguely classical murals, white tablecloths and waiter's black vest tell you this is a nice place. The La Palina model of hospitality apparently stipulates they won't chase you away. At the next table two women were working on wine and dessert when we sat down, and still at it when we left.

→ **159 AVENUE O**

📞 **TEL:** *718 236 9764*

🍴 **SUN, TUE, WED, THU:** *12noon-9.30pm*
  FRI: *12noon-10.30pm*
  SAT: *12noon-11pm*
  FULL BAR

Lenny's Pizza

Opening day for Lenny's was in 1953, but film buffs know it as the place John Travolta stops for a slice in 1977's *Saturday Night Fever*. They offer many exotic pizza permutations, like a grilled chicken Caesar salad slice, a mixed vegetable on a whole wheat crust, and one called a grandpa slice (their spin on the grandma craze). The blasphemers even have a Philly cheese steak! But how are you not going to order two plain slices so you can stack and fold 'em, just like Tony Manero done?

→ **1969 86TH STREET**
☎ TEL: *718 946 1292*

▯ DAILY: *11am-10.30pm*

Lioni's Italian Heroes

For more than 20 years a former mozzarella factory on a sidestreet of Bensonhurst has been home to this exemplar of the Italian sandwich shop. The menu consists of 150 unique variations on the Brooklyn hero, all named after the borough's favourite celebrities; natives like Marisa Tomei and Tony Danza; and immortals who, no fault of their own, were not fortunate enough to be born there, like Frank Sinatra and Dean Martin. Lioni's popularity means the kitchen is a perpetual hive of activity. The scene at the few tables in the front of the store is more relaxed, as regulars linger over enormous sandwiches and kibitz with everyone, neighbourhood pals and strangers alike.

→ 7803 15TH AVENUE

📞 TEL: *718 232 1411*

▯ MON-SAT: *8am-7pm*
SUN: *8.30am-2.30pm*

Ortobello Restaurant

Ortobello is the kind of neighbourhood stalwart the locals flock to year after year. This Bensonhurst red sauce joint opened in 1975 as Gino's and a quick glance around the small dining room tells us almost nothing has changed: marbled mirrors, plastic Tiffany-style hanging lamps, and a Pepsi cooler. It's not cheap, but portions are enormous. Jug wine is served in a goblet, salad in a giant family-sized bowl. Big parties are the norm, and the scene can get a little giddy. Overheard: "You're dropping sauce in my phone!" and "We still got a big chicken parm coming our way!"

→ 6401 BAY PARKWAY

📞 TEL: *718 236 9810*

📱 MON: *4pm-10pm*

TUE-THU: *12noon-3pm & 4pm-10pm*

FRI-SAT: *12noon-3pm & 4pm-11pm*

SUN: *1pm-9pm*

BEER & WINE

CASH REQUESTED FOR GRATUITIES

Pastosa Ravioli

You may find Pastosa fresh ravioli, macaroni and other noodles in their cheerful blue striped boxes at NYC markets but come to the source to stock up on fresh mozzarella, gnocchi, cured meats, olives, oils, vinegars and everything else you'll need for a Brooklyn-style feast. The first Pastosa Ravioli opened in 1966 and has been in this location since 1972. It is run by the third generation of the Ajello family. The multitude of ravioli stuffings is colossal: artichoke, spinach or broccoli rabe; ricotta, goat cheese, or gorgonzola; shrimp, lobster, mushroom, truffle… it can be dizzying.

→ **7425 NEW UTRECHT AVENUE**
☎ **TEL:** *718 236 9615*

▯ **MON:** *11am-6pm*
TUE-SAT: *8am-6pm*
SUN: *8am-2pm*

Rimini Pastry Shoppe

A jewel of an Italian pastry shop, the Rimini has stood on this busy corner since 1973. Owner and baker John Zito learned his trade in Torreta, Sicily. All the classic cookies and pastries you would expect from an Italian bakery are here, as well as coffee and gelato, but their main claim to fame may be cakes; cream pies, cheese cakes and layer cakes of all descriptions fill the windows. At Christmas they do a lively business in holiday gift baskets, overflowing with tri-colour and amaretto cookies, marzipan, and cannoli.

→ **6822 BAY PARKWAY**
☎ **TEL:** *718 236 0644*

▯ **SUN-THU:** *7am-9pm*
FRI-SAT: *7am-9.30pm*

Silver Star

Years ago in much of America there was one kind of Chinese restaurant; nominally Cantonese, the cuisine was actually more American than anything identifiably Asian. Waves of new immigrants have completely remade our ideas about Chinese food. To say the very least, this has been to everyone's benefit. But increasing sophistication has a cost: there is no place left to get a dish of chop suey. Except, that is, the Silver Star, which opened in 1944 and carries on as though nothing notable has happened in the interim. The anachronism begins at the door, where just beyond the cashier's station you pass through a very film-noir wooden arch decorated with dragons and into the dining room, lined on two walls with sparkly-green vinyl upholstered booths. The menu offers such extinct Americanisms as chow mein and chop suey, old favourites like egg drop soup and moo goo gai pan. The crowd loves it, and why not? This is the Chinese food they grew up with.

→ **6221 18TH AVENUE**

📞 **TEL:** *718 331 2799*

📱 **DAILY:** *11am-10.30pm*

Villabate-Alba Pasticceria

In 1979 the Alaimo family bought the Alba Bakery. They added the name of their Sicilian hometown, Villabate, but kept the Alba out of respect for a business that had been a neighbourhood favourite since 1935. Nearly 40 years later this pasticceria is more popular than ever. You will find not one, but two lines for service; one headed for their made-fresh gelati, another for pastries, cookies, cannolis, grain pies, you get the picture. Devoted fans who are former Bensonhurst residents — and many of their descendants — still flock here, especially at the holidays.

→ 7001 18TH AVENUE

☎ TEL: *718 331 8430*

▯ DAILY: *7am-9pm*

Bari Pork Store

In Mapleton or scenic Gravesend, this is the "king of the sausage". Bari is a full service butcher, and there is also a deli counter for heroes and pre-made dishes like eggplant rollatini. They have been in business since 1967 offering practically anything you desire for a proper antipasto, from fresh mozzarella and bocconcini to a vast array of imported tidbits and delicacies. If tchotchkes are your thing, feast your eyes on a collection of comic ceramic pigs while you wait for your order. And if you are on your way to a dinner party the Avenue U store will sell you flowers to please your host, as if the armload of cold cuts you bring wouldn't do the trick.

→ 158 AVENUE U
☎ TEL: *718 372 6405*

→ 6319 18TH AVE
☎ TEL: *718 837 9773*

🖥 MON-SAT: *8am-6.30pm,*
SUN: *8am-2pm*

Cuccio's Bakery

An Italian bakery with hamantaschen in the window? A little flexibility doesn't hurt when keeping your 1937-vintage business relevant to a changing neighbourhood. It can't all be biscotti and seven-layer cookies. To cover all the bases, they also make Irish soda bread and linzer tarts. Then there are pies, specialty cakes, nut clusters and other sweets. Breads range from Italian to rye, pumpernickel and challah. The evolving diversity of styles has been a strength of Cuccio's many decades, but a high quality product is the main reason they are still a vital part of Gravesend.

→ 320 AVENUE X

☎ TEL: *718 336 1944*

🗓 MON-SAT: *7am-7.45pm*
  SUN: *7am-6.45pm*
  CASH ONLY

Donut Shoppe aka Shaikh's Place

This small, unassuming luncheonette offers some of the best doughnuts in New York City. They're incredibly fresh and puffy, full of flavour (the chocolate tastes of rich cocoa), and scented with the lightest most beautiful bakery perfume. Get a seat at the small counter (if you can – the place is busy) for a hamburger, quesadilla, or a plate of meat over rice. And buy some more doughnuts to take home, so later you'll have no regrets.

→ 1503 AVENUE U
📞 TEL: *718 375 2572*

🗓 DAILY: *24 hours*
CASH ONLY

Joe's of Avenue U

Not the '70s diner it would appear at first glance, Joe's is a Focacceria Palermitana, meaning they specialise in Sicilian dishes and they have been doing it since the 1960s. Take their panelle, delicately fried chickpea fritters, offered as a side dish or sandwich on a round roll. Best is the special panelle, topped with ricotta. Other Palermo pick hits include a vastedda sandwich for the spleen fans, or polpo and calamari salad, if tentacles grab you. Another rarity is sardi a beccafico, sardine roll-ups stuffed with breadcrumbs, pine nuts, raisins and parsley. On your way into the seating area, have a good long look at the many prepared dishes displayed in a long counter. Whether that will help you decide what to order, or not, it's a good appetiser.

→   **287 AVENUE U**

📞   **TEL:** *718 449 9285*

🕐   **MON-SAT:** *11am-8.30pm*
    SUN: *11am-7.30pm*

L&B Spumoni Gardens

A legend and a landmark, the 1950s-vintage L&B Spumoni Gardens needs no introduction to pizza fanatics. Their fame is built on a Sicilian pizza baked in the old-fashioned "upside down" style, with the cheese next to the crust and the sauce on top. You can buy a square, but most customers order a whole or half tray. It is thick, saucy, and slightly undercooked which lends a markedly doughy texture. How this slice doesn't sit on your stomach like a cinder block is a mystery, but it is much lighter than it looks. Spumoni Gardens is actually a complex of three buildings: pizzeria, ice cream shop and dining room, whose origins go back to a horse-drawn cart Ludovico Barbati used to sell pizza in the neighbourhood. In 1939 they built a small spumoni ice cream factory, adding the pizzeria in the 1950s. It is perpetually busy; in summer the garden picnic tables are always full of families waiting for a pie.

→ 2725 86TH STREET

☎ TEL: *718 449 1230*

▯ SEASONAL HOURS, WILL BE SHORTER IN WINTER
SUN-THU: *11am-12midnight* FRI-SAT: *11am-1am*
BEER & WINE

SEASIDE

6

Gargiulo's Italian Restaurant

It's not all hot dogs and clam strips in Coney Island. For a sit-down, dressed up, Neopolitan dinner you go to elegant Gargiulo's. The exterior gives the impression of a banquet hall, but have faith. Sadly, the lobby and bar had to be fully rebuilt following the devastation of Hurricane Sandy in 2012, but inside is a less ornate version of what must have met one's eyes in 1907, Coney Island's heyday, and Gargiulo's first year. The potted palms remain. Attentive service by career waiters in tuxedos. When you ask for the check you become a part of an old tradition at Gargiulo's: betting on the check. The waiter produces a conical vessel called the tombola, and asks for a number. If he shakes that out of the tombola, dinner is free. If not? You can't always win, sometimes you lose.

→ **2911 W 15TH STREET**

📞 **TEL:** *718 266 4891*

▯ **MON, WED, THU:** *12noon-10.30pm*
FRI-SAT: *12noon-11.30pm*
SUN: *12noon-9.30pm*
FULL BAR
PROPER ATTIRE REQUIRED

Nathan's Famous

Nathan's practically invented the hot dog as we know it (though they say a fellow named Feltman first put sausage to bun in Coney Island back in 1871), so order one — not just for history's sake (Nathan's has already passed its centennial); it is a great dog. We've always been big fans of the fries, crinkle-cut and well-done, and you don't want to miss out on the fried clam strips or shrimp. The scene on a sunny weekend is bound to be chaotic, so it is important to remember that there are dedicated lines for different foods: a line for seafood, another for hot dogs. Stick with it, the reward is worth it.

→ 1310 SURF AVENUE

☎ TEL: *718 946 2202*

🖥 SUN-THU: *9am-1am*
FRI-SAT: *9am-2am*
BEER ON TAP

Paul's Daughter

Brothers Gregory and Paul Georgoulakos opened their seaside snack bar in in 1962. Like the name suggests, it is now run by Paul's daughter, Tina. They managed to come back from the mass eviction in 2009, the work of evil landlord skullduggery that threatened so many boardwalk businesses. After a much needed renovation that thankfully has not diminished its charm, Paul's is again serving clams on the halfshell, sausage and peppers heroes, and wads of cotton candy to crowds of sandy Coney Island revellers.

→ 1001 RIEGELMANN BOARDWALK

☎ TEL: *718 449 4252*

▯ LIKE EVERYTHING IN CONEY ISLAND, HOURS VARY SEASONALLY.
BEER ON TAP

Ruby's Bar & Grill

There is no better way to enjoy the Coney Island board-walk craziness than from a barstool at Ruby's, beer in hand, shaded from the sun, cooled by the ocean breeze. The air is redolent of fried food and sea salt, and the jukebox is blasting golden oldie teenage rock'n'roll. After a redevelopment scare threatened to shut it for good it's been gussied up a bit, but it's still the same old Ruby's. A bar since 1934 and owned by the same family since 1975, Ruby's is now the oldest on the boardwalk. There is a full bar and if you need a nosh, a menu of seaside favourites like fried clams and shrimp, or for the landlubbers perhaps a corndog or burger.

→ **1213 RIEGELMANN BOARDWALK**

☎ **TEL:** *718 975 7829*

▯ **SEASONAL HOURS**
SUN-THU: *11am-10pm*
FRI-SAT: *11am-1am*

Totonno's

This dear old pizzeria dating from 1924 is a Coney Island institution as faithfully revered as the Cyclone roller coaster (Totonno's junior by three years). They don't sell slices, only pies, so bring friends or a large appetite. The pizza is a classic New York pie, thin crust with a substantial outer edge well-decorated with charred bits and bubbles. Sauce and fresh mozzarella, top quality both, might exist chiefly as an excuse to eat that crust. Tin ceilings and walls are flat white, wooden booths painted black, it's like walking into an old photo album. There is no canned music, but you will be serenaded by the dulcet tones of your proprietress, Cookie, sorting out the intricacies of managing a pizza joint in a voice hard enough to drive nails. Beer and wine are available. Coca Cola in glass bottles, and an East Coast favourite, Stewart's brand sodas, add to the old-time atmosphere.

→ 1524 NEPTUNE AVENUE

📞 TEL: *718 372 8606*

▣ THU–SUN: *12noon-7.30pm*
   CASH ONLY
   BEER & WINE

Williams Candy

From their opening in 1936, nothing has stopped Williams Candy catering to Coney Island's sweet tooth, though Hurricane Sandy came close. Peter Agrapides, owner for the last three decades, and a Williams Candy fan for more than 60 years, had some serious rebuilding to do after that epic storm. Yet step through the door and it's like nothing has changed. It still feels like entering a candy cloud, the contact sugar rush providing an instant lift to the spirit, destroying any sales resistance. Caramel apples, jelly apples, crazy candied marshmallow treats on skewers, popcorn balls and cotton candy — it's every childhood stomach ache you ever had, and you are powerless before its siren song.

→ **1318 SURF AVENUE**

☎ **TEL:** *718 372 0302*

📱 **SUN-THU:** *10am-7pm*
   FRI-SAT: *9am-7pm*

Jordan's Lobster Dock

Between the Belt Parkway and Plumb Beach Channel sits this seafood house. The Jordan family has been in the seafood biz since 1938, and at this location since 1966. There is a retail fish market at the back, and in the front a restaurant. The style is order-at-the-counter fast food, with a dining area with wood tables and chairs. A red and white cardboard container of big fat Ipswich clams, fried, will make you completely forget there's a TGI Friday's next door. There are clams and oysters on the half shell, Maine lobster rolls, and combo plates of fish, shrimp or crab. New England clam chowder is excellent, the coleslaw is free, and there's Brooklyn Lager on tap.

→ 3165 HARKNESS AVENUE

📞 TEL: *1 800 404 CLAW*

🕐 SUN-THU: *11am-9pm*
FRI-SAT: *11am-10.30pm*
BEER & WINE

Tamaqua Bar & Marina

If you don't have wheels, getting to Gerritsen Beach on public transport will be a chore. It is literally a backwater of the borough, tucked up behind Breezy Point, and strictly for locals and hardcore boaters. Three generations of Sarubbis have run this marina, starting in 1934. Sure, you can dock a boat here, but the best part of any marina should be the bar. This is a spacious barn of a place with a rectangular centre bar, more than adequate for the crowd of regulars. Giant fishing trophies — marlin, a hammerhead shark — decorate the walls, but if you want fish stories, your drinking companions will supply them. Hang around for a bit and Patty the bartender may park a big tray of cheese and sopressata in front of you.

→ **84 EBONY COURT**

📞 **TEL:** *718 646 9212*

🗓 **DAILY:** *8am-12midnight*

Landi's Pork Store

The stunningly beautiful, perfectly intact, blue and white metal storefront announcing Landi's Pork Store welcomes shoppers to this enduringly popular market, a pride of the neighbourhood. Landi's has had a long history in Brooklyn, first downtown on Navy Street, later on Myrtle Avenue; 1959 was the opening of this final location. Peer through the plate glass window and see how the proverbial sausage is made. The butcher's block and delicatessen take up one side, the far counter is for prepared food; frozen sauces and pre-made pasta dishes await to "heat & serve" at home. Weekend crowds are bedlam, and you don't want to be in here on Christmas Eve.

→ 5909 AVENUE N
📞 TEL: *718 763 3230*

📱 MON–SAT: *8am–6pm*
SUN: *9am–2pm*

Mill Basin Kosher Deli

If you are in the Jewish deli business you know the value of tradition. Since 1973 Mill Basin Deli has honoured that, serving huge portions of succulent corned beef and pastrami, pickles and coleslaw that are good enough to be an entree on their own. From an egg cream to matzoh ball soup, all the hits are here. But let's not get too stuffy, there's also a little whimsy in the menu. Like the PLT, where fried pastrami takes the place of bacon in a BLT, or a pastrami egg roll. Surrealists might appreciate the Hush Puppy, a potato knish impaled on a hot dog. Speaking of art, in another unexpected twist, the walls are covered with the owner's name-brand art collection (all for sale).

→ 5823 AVENUE T

☎ TEL: *718 241 4910*

▥ MON-THU: *9am-9pm*
   FRI-SAT: *9am-10pm*
   SUN: *9am-9.30pm*
   FULL BAR

Brennan & Carr

There is an argument to be made for simplicity in the restaurant business, one that Brennan & Carr has been successfully advocating since 1938. Apparently loathe to dissipate their energy on being all things to all people, they strive to do a few things very well. The menu is small enough to fit on the left half of the paper placemat. The main event is a hot roast beef sandwich, served rare on a hard roll dipped in beef broth. There are alternatives: a grilled chicken sandwich or a burger if you must, fries or onion rings for a side. If you can't settle for less than too much, order a Gargiulo burger, a cheeseburger topped with roast beef and grilled onions. If this sounds like a mess, you may be right aesthetically, but it's also delicious. The odd-shaped low building located at a crossroads suggests a genuine roadhouse, once a standard type of restaurant, now rare as hen's teeth. A part of Brennan & Carr will always be 1938: white jackets on waiters, the pine paneling on the walls, clam chowder, beef broth, and pie a la mode on the menu.

→ **3432 NOSTRAND AVENUE**

☏ **TEL:** *718 769 1254*

▯ **DAILY:** *11am-12midnight*

Randazzo's Clam Bar

Across the street from a line of excursion fishing boats docked in Sheepshead Bay is the last of the old-time seafood joints on Emmons Avenue, Randazzo's, once a fishmonger and bar, once a formal restaurant, and once destroyed by Hurricane Sandy. The old-time ambience comes from lifetime customers returning again and again for Randazzo's Brooklyn-style Italian-American seafood in a diner-like setting: start with littlenecks or cherrystones on the half shell and then move on to scungilli (aka conch, aka whelk, aka those chewy rubber eraser things) or some fried seafood with Randazzo's hot or mild tomato sauce. At the sign of the neon lobster.

→ 2017 EMMONS AVENUE

📞 TEL: *718 615 0010*

🖥 MON–THU: *11am-11pm*
FRI–SUN: *11am-12midnight*
BEER & WINE

Roll N Roaster

Ever wonder what Arby's would be like if they served food that was edible? On Mars? This Sheepshead Bay landmark has been dishing up roast beef sandwiches since 1970 with all the honky-tonk of a gigantic fast food chain, but it's strictly one-of-a-kind. The seats are just as hard, and the worker's uniforms as humiliating as any Burger King's, but the food has none of the plastic 1984-ishness of the multinational competition. Spring for a 50¢ side of pickles to pep up your gravy-dipped roast beef with grilled onions; the sweet potato fries make a nice accompaniment. Marvel at the acid trip Spanish Gothic '70s timewarp decor. The bibulous will be happy to see that unlike most fast food joints, alcohol is on the menu; very affordable lager and splits of unsurprisingly dodgy wine, but we can only imagine the sort of high-roller who orders the $59.99 bottle of Moët. To set the mood, check YouTube to screen one of Roll N Roaster's ultra-cheesy vintage television ads.

→ 2901 EMMONS AVENUE

☎ TEL: *718 769 6000*

🗓 SUN-THU: *11am-1am* FRI-SAT: *11am-3am*
 BEER AND WINE

INDEX

Entries by neighbourhood

Entries
A-Z

About **Herb Lester**

Founded in 2010, Herb Lester Associates have brought a fresh voice to the familiar. Their beautifully designed guides sidestep famous landmarks and flash-in-the-pan fads in favour of a more beguiling world around the next corner.

Carefully researched and highly opinionated, the guides highlight the best of new and old; out of the way bars, overlooked eating places, hidden parks, specialist shops, museums and galleries.

Most guides try to tell the reader everything there is to know about a place, Herb Lester Associates just tell you how to enjoy it.

HERBLESTER.COM

About **the authors**

Jon Hammer and Karen McBurnie distill and decant the best of New York City at Grade "A" Fancy. Their books include Hark! The Radio Bartender Brings and Code Name: Cocktail (with Vicky Sweat). They are also co-creators of NYC and DC gadabout city maps published by Herb Lester.

GRADE-A-FANCY-MAGAZINE.COM